Where Magic Wears a Red Hat – The Art of Stanley Murphy

Where Magic Wears a Red Hat
The Art of Stanley Murphy

MARTHA'S VINEYARD HISTORICAL SOCIETY 2004

First published by Martha's Vineyard
Historical Society 2004

"Where Magic Wears a Red Hat —
The Art of Stanley Murphy"
© Karal Ann Marling 2004

All works by Stanley Murphy
© Estate of Stanley Murphy 2004

Martha's Vineyard Historical Society
P.O. Box 1310
Edgartown, Massachusetts 02539

ISBN 0-9665253-3-7

Printed and bound in China

Acknowledgment is gratefully
offered to the owners of the works
reproduced in this volume and
to members of the Murphy family;
to Christopher Morse, Ann K. Nelson,
and Amor H. Towles; and to Matthew
Stackpole, Director of the Martha's
Vineyard Historical Society, and
Stephen Borkowski, Chairman of the
Provincetown Art Commission.

Design: Lorraine Ferguson
Editor: Janet Jenkins
Editorial Assistance: Jennifer Uhrhane

Photography by Ron Hall,
unless otherwise noted.
Frank Graham: pp. 61, 91, front jacket.
Robert E. Mates: p. 14.
Alison Shaw: p. 94.
James Zimmerman: p. 12.

The descriptions that accompany
each work in the color plates
are adapted from original captions
written by the Murphy family.
These captions appeared as wall
texts for the exhibition *Fifty Years
of Island Portraits,* mounted in Chilmark,
Massachusetts, in August 2002.
The medium for each painting is
given as recorded by the artist;
variation between use of the terms
"board," "panel," and "wood"
is preserved. Dimensions are given
in inches; height precedes width.

Frontispiece
Self-Portrait in Red Hat 1978
oil on panel
24 × 18
Collection Polly Woollcott Murphy

Foreword

ROBERT W. DORAN

7

Where Magic Wears a Red Hat — The Art of Stanley Murphy

KARAL ANN MARLING

11

The Plates

21

Artist's Chronology

94

David and Sunshine 2002
oil on canvas
38 × 50
Private collection

Foreword

In late August 2002, Stanley Murphy asked me to write an introduction for a book to document the acclaimed exhibition of his portraits that had just ended. The show had been a vintage Vineyard happening, drawing a large and enthusiastic crowd. "But Stan," I protested when he asked me, "I'm neither a writer nor an art critic." "Perfect," he replied, "you will do it, then."

The retrospective exhibition *Fifty Years of Island Portraits,* which this book, at last, commemorates, had been the idea of Polly Murphy, Stan's wife. Members of the family wrote the short, informal captions that accompanied the paintings, and none of the works were for sale. Many of the individuals whose portraits were shown attended the exhibition in person: it was fascinating to see the paintings and the people they portrayed staring at one another in the same space. And it was altogether fitting that the exhibition took place in the Stanley Murphy Gallery.

The gallery is a fixture on Martha's Vineyard. It sits back from the road in a field just over the Chilmark line, the artist's name hammered out in large galvanized nails on the side of the shacklike building. Here Stan held his first show in 1958, and from that point on exhibitions of his work took place every year (and later, every other year) starting in early July. The paintings—still lifes, landscapes, seascapes, and portraits—would hang in the gallery for the summer months, and the buyers would pick them up on Labor Day. The gallery is small and the space not really ideal for the display of art, but that didn't prevent Stan's admirers from showing up. And they showed up religiously. At each of the openings they would be greeted by a tent that had been erected just outside the gallery, where a group would gather to pay respects to the Murphy family, eat Chilmark Chocolates, and wait for the door to open.

My first connection to Stan was through these exhibitions and through his work. Beginning about twenty-five years ago, my wife, Happy, and I were among those who waited impatiently under the sparkling white tent. There was something tense about those moments just before four o'clock. A number of us would gradually work our way closer to the door to assure being among the first to see and acquire the artist's recent paintings. We would then rush in and fan out in the tight space. We especially liked coming back during the hot days of August, when things were quiet and the gallery empty except for family. It was during those visits that we got to know the family and, ultimately, to meet Stan.

One of the delights of collecting works of art is the opportunity to get to know the artist. In Stan's case, this took quite a while. Our relationship developed very slowly and deepened over the years. Happy and I would visit the Murphy house, work our way past the dogs, and settle in for a quiet chat with Stan and Polly. The introduction to the artist we had first received through his paintings ultimately developed into a close personal relationship. As the years passed, we were increasingly grateful for that relationship.

If I were asked to characterize Stan, I would say he was a soft-spoken, private person. I never heard him raise his voice, and he seemed always to speak with a smile. Yet at the same time, I found him to be fiercely independent, stubborn, driven, and proud. We wrote letters to each other, and our relationship was enhanced through the written word. I recall writing him about whether he might consider coming to the portrait exhibition. His reply was typical Murphy: "Maybe I will, and maybe I won't." Stan had once told me he didn't want to hear what people had to say at his openings; it was one of the reasons he famously stayed away. To my surprise, he did attend that show—the first in fifty years. At the end of the evening, he insisted we stop by his house to see a portrait he had just finished. Standing in the driveway, he confessed that he was glad he had attended—that he only wished he had tape-recorded what people had said to him. After half a century and very near the end of his life, the artist who had devoted a career to recording the people among whom he lived and worked at last reached out to listen to their reactions, and wished he could record those, too. This book, in a sense, is a tribute to that penultimate realization of the artist: a public record of a long-private man.

Other talented Vineyard artists respected Stan, and I liked what they said about his work.

One of them wrote to me:

Without knowing the people in his portraits directly, I still feel I have met them. Their lives and work expand my knowledge of and connection to this Island. If Martha's Vineyard were a fabric, Stan's threads would crisscross through it and make it very strong. I overheard someone say the other day that Stan was "genuine," and to me that's the ultimate compliment, and probably the reason Stan's paintings are impossible to confuse with anyone else's.

Another Island artist, a portrait of whom was in the exhibition, understood the work's immediacy this way:

To do a self-portrait, you have to know yourself … and you have to do self-portraits before you can capture the essence of others.

Stan knew himself and, ultimately, his work. Several months before he died, he surprised me one day, confiding that he wished to be recognized as a "master" some day. He had confidence enough in his art near the end of his career that he thought it should be acknowledged more broadly, at last; but he wondered out loud if it would ever happen. Many of us have long felt Stanley Murphy was a master. They were among those who attended the extraordinary memorial service held in his honor under a tent in the field behind the Murphy house alongside a glistening pond. The setting was incredibly beautiful. Mysteriously, as if staged for a portrait, in the row after row of chairs that had been set out, no chair was empty and no one was left standing. It was like so many things about Stan's work … just right. The format was unusual: sixteen speakers introduced themselves, some speaking as family members, others simply as friends, and still others as artists and collectors. The range of speakers and the various sentiments they expressed highlighted the breadth of his relationships and the depth of the feelings he inspired. Each stood and spoke warmly of the man and glowingly of his talent. No one wanted it to end.

I often wish that Stan were here so I could ask him about one painting or another: what he thought of this subject, why he chose that particular setting, this particular color. And I can picture him after I've asked my questions. He is sitting in his high-back chair, smiling quietly to himself, reflecting, in no particular hurry. He is wondering if he should answer. And no doubt he is thinking that maybe he will and maybe he won't.

ROBERT W. DORAN

Keith's Farm with Ozzie Fischer 1972
oil on panel
32 x 50
Collection Chilmark Library

Where Magic Wears a Red Hat
The Art of Stanley Murphy

KARAL ANN MARLING

Suddenly, during the 1880s and 90s, after more than two hundred years of pioneer plundering, Americans discovered something beautiful in places left behind when the nation drove westward chasing gold, free land, and big dreams. Suddenly, little dreams—dreams of quiet yesterdays and black shutters on wooden houses and people who worked with their hands and their hearts—began to soothe the fretful sleep of urbanites, caught up in a frenzy of noise, squalor, competition, and isolation.

Along the Eastern seaboard, writers, painters, actors, rebels, and hacks—and a new crop of plain-old summer vacationers—discovered towns that modern progress seemed to have left behind. Woodstock, in the Rip Van Winkle–haunted Catskill Mountains, where the tanning industry had faltered and farming had never amounted to much in the first place. Old Lyme, in Connecticut, with its stately colonial mansions tottering into genteel decay. Provincetown, Rockport, Ogunquit, Gloucester, where whalers once berthed and fishermen still plied their lonely, dangerous trade.

The appeal to tourists was fresh air, the low prices for room and board, and the patented quaintness of the American peasantry—the unregimented worker in his oilskins and overalls, who lived all year round on a narrow, crooked street, in a house his great-great-grandfather might have built. Rockport and Old Lyme and the rest weren't modern. Even though the Provincetown fleet reached the high point of its profitability in 1885, to the eye of the urbanite, the economics of fishing were irrelevant to the charm of places where homemade berry pies still cooled on windowsills and a young art student could get a nice room, three squares a day, and laundry for six dollars a week.

Charles W. Hawthorne
The Crew of the Philomena Manta 1915–16
oil on canvas
75 ½ x 92 ½
Collection Town of Provincetown
Courtesy Provincetown Art Commission

The artists who came along with the tourists reflected their interests. The pictures the summer folk took home with them showed the old houses, the sandy beaches, the local characters. Charles Hawthorne (1872–1930), founder of the Cape Cod School of Art who came to Provincetown in the late 1800s, made the Portuguese fishermen and their families his primary subject. One of his best-known works, *The Crew of the Philomena Manta* (1915–16), shows a group of stolid fishermen, young and old, returning with their catch. Seen from above, in their oilskins, amid the tools of their trade, they fill the canvas completely, except for a gap right above a basket overflowing with fish. The result is a solemn, almost sacramental paean to the virtue, the authenticity, and the heroism of hard, demanding work.

It comes as a shock, then, to learn that there was no such boat: Hawthorne thought the name sounded right! As for the crew, it was made up of three of his pupils, some lumberyard hands, a gardener, and only one genuine fisherman. But, in the end, the picture is exactly right. It tells the story that summers along the shoreline of New England told to those who went in search of honesty, simplicity, and courage. He painted old sea captains and their crews, the local selectmen in council, aging women with wise eyes and hard, capable hands, and young boys bound for the sea. He painted subjects redolent of a prim, tough American Eden, a sort of Yankee paradise: simpler times and plain, uncluttered places.

In July of 1920, as the first discordant notes of the Jazz Age sounded in New York City, a young painter originally from Missouri—Thomas Hart Benton (1889–1975)—came to the island of Martha's Vineyard for the summer, full of arcane theory and enthusiasm for "modern" art. He lived in the barn behind Ella Brug's boardinghouse in Chilmark that season, in hot pursuit of a devoted guest who would shortly become his wife. By 1927, the Bentons had settled in for good as summer Islanders, not far from the South Road camp where a motley assortment of Union Square radicals and intellectuals gathered for sunlight and long, stimulating drafts of locally made moonshine. Van Wyck Brooks, Eugene Debs, Walter Lippmann, Norman Thomas, Thomas Craven, Lewis Mumford, and Bernard de Voto came and went while Benton slowly but surely absorbed something of this spare, lovely place.

The Chilmark end of the Vineyard became for Benton the moral equivalent of the Ozarks of his youth, isolated and steeped in the old ways. Settled in the early seventeenth century (in 1668 the governor bought a large tract of land on the South Road from a tribal sachem for "a cow and a suit of clothes from top to toe and seventeen pounds in money"), Chilmark was still populated in the 1920s by the descendants of the original settlers. They made the same meager living their ancestors had made, by a little farming, a little fishing, some herding, some woodcutting. Hereditary deafness afflicted half the population, which harbored more than its fair share of self-willed, rustic eccentrics, including moonshiners and a farmer reputed to strain the milk he sold to summer guests through his own ancient, much-used pocket handkerchief.

With the exception of a few Cubist-influenced beach scenes painted early in the decade, most of Tom Benton's summer pictures from 1920 until his death in 1975 dealt with Vineyard natives and their haunts. Although he was sometimes accused of being a perpetual tourist, who dropped in on picturesque aspects of the American Scene for brief moments and then scurried on to new ones, from the beginning Benton aimed to understand and to honor the neighbors he painted on the Vineyard.

The Lord Is My Shepherd (1926) is a case in point, a portrait of George West and his wife, Sabrina, seated at their kitchen table over the evening meal in the summer of 1922. The Wests, both deaf (as were two of their three children), lived not far from the Brug barn, in the vicinity of Beetlebung Corner; they were Tom's neighbors, in other words. He describes their hardworking lives by exaggerating the size of their hands, momentarily at rest among the simple accoutrements of the table. The stillness of the figures and the written text of the sampler on the wall behind them suggest a world of silence, but so does the monumental stillness of the bare, orderly scene. The meal becomes a sacrament, a tribute to God-fearing people who earn their bread by unremitting physical labor.

In the 1960s, reminiscing about the subjects of his paintings and prints, Benton remembered each of his Vineyard scenes with a particularity that points to a deep knowledge of and respect for the Islanders. This was Henry Look's white calf, he said. That was a hand scythe used by reapers in the small, irregular fields of the Vineyard. Here's the farm of Denys Wortman, "famous New York newspaper cartoonist." There's Gale Huntington, Chilmark folk singer and history and Latin teacher, making music with his little daughter, Emily. A picture of his own daughter, Jesse, posed as Little Red Riding Hood in the Benton woodlot, prompts his observation that Vineyard trees are peculiarly broad near the roots because the constant wind stunts their upward growth. Fairytale. Folk wisdom. Old whalers' ditties. Hard work. Fathers and daughters. Martha's Vineyard.

Enter Stanley Murphy (1922–2003), fresh from an unsatisfactory course of study in graphics and commercial art under the G.I. Bill at New York's Art Students League. As he told the story, the former army lieutenant wandered into the Frick Gallery one day and experienced a blinding moment of epiphany in front of a Rembrandt self-portrait. While art schools were abuzz with the triumphs of Abstract Expressionism and Jackson Pollock wannabes haunted Madison Avenue, Murphy found himself drawn to the human content of Rembrandt and the Flemish masters. But how to duplicate their luminous effects? There was nobody willing to teach him the techniques of Bruegel's glazing and underpainting in drip-mad New York, nor were his teachers sympathetic to a young man who wanted to paint actual pictures of people and their environments in the heady, nonobjective world of the late 1940s.

Like Benton, Stan Murphy was smitten with a girl, Polly Woollcott, who spent her summers on Martha's Vineyard. By 1948, he had moved there with Polly and their baby son. This was no warm-weather flirtation with Island living, however. The Murphys had come to stay. From books on the Old Masters and lots of painful experimentation, Stan taught himself to paint the way he thought it ought to be done; he later lamented the fact that he'd lost ten long years working out what a good instructor ought to have been able to teach an apprentice in no time at all. But maybe Stan's way was the best way.

Jackson Pollock had studied with Benton right there on the Island in the 1930s and had been so much in awe of his teacher that his early paintings looked like copies of the older man's work. Stan befriended Benton years afterward, as a fellow Vineyard artist, and bristled at the suggestion that his pictures looked anything like old Tom's. "We were good friends," Murphy said. "For a long time he was the only professional painter I knew on the Island. I loved him. I would come home from his house filled to the brim, but for somebody to liken my paintings to his is ridiculous." And yet, despite Stan

Murphy's denial, there's something in the comparison—perhaps a shared interest in character, a curiosity about the lives of others, a love for a place and its people.

Unlike his friend Tom's work, however, Stan Murphy's art is that of a portraitist, who carves the faces of his neighbors with a fond determination, out of some unknown, obdurate substance: The glacial boulders on which they sit? The rocks of the walls that surround their fields? The ice glistening beneath a fisherman's catch? The chromed steel radiator of a big rig? The weathered shingles of the West Tisbury Town Office? The gleaming red fenders of the volunteers' fire truck? And the portraits are not simply of the people of Martha's Vineyard. There's a pair of oxen, a flutter of birds, a cow named Sunshine, a dog named Charity, a crow named Harrison, fishes of every sort, a dead duck, a cat, and a stubborn little poodle, all treated with the same painstaking, stroke-by-stroke earnestness. They're there, present and accounted for, it seems, for all eternity, in their foul-weather gear, their suspenders, their billed caps, in a world of animals, golden fields, and vast blue seas.

The palpable effort of the artist manifest in every portrait—the work of mind and eye and hand—matches the engagement of the sitter. In this meticulous approach to the reality of his subject, Stan Murphy parts company with Benton and with the painters of his own generation. His is the timeless art of the primitive, the self-taught limner whose aim is nothing less than an ultimate truth to which issues of style or fashion are profoundly irrelevant. Murphy never missed an opportunity to see exhibitions of great art: Picasso, Cézanne, Matisse, and Marsden Hartley, whose tough New England landscapes must have struck a resonant chord. But at the end of the day, Murphy was Murphy, the man who carved portraits in paint with the same laconic honesty that he admired in the old craftsmen whose duck decoys he studied and celebrated.

Because Murphy could not support his growing family on art alone during his first years on the Island, he worked, as the Islanders themselves did, at a variety of odd jobs. At Hancock's Hardware, he stocked shelves and made blueprints. He labored on Everett Whiting's farm. He helped with construction projects for Tom Waldron. Ernest Mayhew, Dan Larsen, and Robert Flanders taught him how to set lobster pots. And he went clamming and hunted ducks, all to put food on the Murphy table. He wore Badge No. 4 as an inaugural member of the West Tisbury Fire Department. He played golf and the piano. He was active in the Martha's Vineyard Historical Society. He opened the second-oldest Vineyard art gallery just over the Chilmark line in 1958, where his own pictures were sold. He was, in short, every inch the Islander, who happened to be a painter. Stan Murphy always called himself a painter, emphasizing the craftsmanlike aspects of his work; whether or not he was an artist, he said, was for others to judge.

In the late 1940s, he had traveled around the Island, knocking at the doors of the fancy houses in hopes that the summer visitors might commission a portrait of the house. And he painted people, too. Both subjects demanded the gimlet-eyed scrutiny of a carpenter, a fireman, a hunter, or a judge of a good crop. And from the beginning, the portrait—a painstaking map or blueprint of personality—was his medium. Portraits "came easily to me," Murphy once told a reporter. But the fact was that he took two months or more for each one of them, often demanding repeated sittings on the part of the subject to get to the nub of reality. "What is it about the human face?" Murphy asked in 1994. "There is a line I have somewhere—I will find it and read it to you exactly, but it goes like this: 'The human face is something which is the greatest history in the world.'" Faces were histories. Faces told wonderful stories.

The most ordinary of men and women are the heroes of these painterly tales, vested with a nobility and sometimes a touch of strangeness as they stand there, returning the fearless scrutiny of Stanley Murphy.

A case in point is Murphy's portrait of Hershel West and his poodle, Minnie, painted in 1994 (p. 83). Hershel, in a shockingly red shirt, tugs at a bright blue crate of ice with his left hand but has stopped for a kind of eternal moment, facing Stan Murphy. The wall over his right shoulder is inscribed with the fisherman's name and that of his dog. The New England portrait painters of colonial times did the same thing, to affirm the existence of this man, in this spot, with this dog (or deer, or prancing steed), to attest to the truth of the image. Under Murphy's gaze, Hershel West becomes an instant ancestor, a piece of history, a validation of Wests and dogs and fishing for generations to come.

Hershel West is history, as real and alive as the hot frisson of red in the coolness of the picture. In 1994, West (along with Minnie) attended an opening at Murphy's gallery dressed just as he had been in the painting, as if to prove that his essential self—the distilled essence of his person—now and forever resided on the canvas. In 1994, according to the current owner of the work, the box contained only ice, beautifully painted, crystalline and glittering. But Stan often, after careful reflection, revisited paintings and changed things. Hence the fish. More local color? A quasi-religious contrast to the poodle: the living and the dead? A part of the parable of the loaves and fishes? Of the eternal struggle to wrest a living from the sea?

Captain Jim Morgan, who fished out of Menemsha for many years (and sometimes painted seascapes himself), posed for Murphy in 1994 aboard the dragger *Mary and Verna,* in shocking yellow oilskins and a red cap, dangling a single, fresh-caught flounder from one hand (p. 79). The simplicity of the color—blue, red, yellow, orange, white—has the finality of hard-won fact. The sea is as deep and unyielding as the gaze of the fisherman. When Morgan saw the painting, he is supposed to have remarked, "Nice flounder, Stan!" The portrait is as terse as Morgan's understated praise.

For all the factual content of a Murphy portrait, however, there lurks beneath that veneer a core of mystery and fantasy. Why is West presenting that single fish, arranged like a jewel on a bed of diamonds? The sea behind Captain Morgan: is it a terrible void or alive with flounder yet uncaught? And why does this one big fish stop the captain in his tracks? One of Murphy's most enigmatic paintings depicts *Laura and Kitty on the Path to Bannie's* (1955, p. 29). Like a Grant Wood landscape, this one resembles a soft, sheltering quilt, a memory quilt made up of squares of yellow and green worsted, cut from hand-me-down coats. Along one seam run two little girls, Stan and Polly's daughters.

He began the picture while they lay in the hospital, desperately ill with Rocky Mountain spotted fever. "When … I knew they were going to live, I came home and made that painting," he remembered. What seem to be fabrics are dense forests and hayfields, arranged in two-dimensional patterns, broken only by a stand of five wispy trees that might have been embroidered into place and by the exuberant gestures of the tiny figures, fairly bursting from the hay. It is a fantasy, a vision of joy, harmony, and perpetual childhood. The real dissolves into the timeless magic of the imagination.

This is the essential paradox of Stanley Murphy's work: how can people and places so real, so present to the eye, also exist as parables, fantasies, and histories? In *The Selectmen of West Tisbury* (1977, p. 55) three men pause on the steps of Town Hall: Allen Look, Everett Whiting, John Alley. Pots of flowers. The American flag. The white painted frame of the doorway. The bright red surface of the door itself. These could be three Byzantine saints about to enter heaven, or a trio of Founding Fathers about to sign the Declaration of Independence. They transcend their own blue work shirts and red vests in a way that Charles Hawthorne's Provincetown selectmen never quite manage to do.

Murphy's picture of five West Tisbury firemen (p. 31), painted twenty years before, is a far less polished piece but gives off the same aura of vast significance as the men confront the viewer, almost daring the outsider to seek admission to their company. All of Stan Murphy's group portraits, with their shallow spaces and stoic, hieratic figures, act as history paintings in which the actors are sealed away in a dimension all their own, an impenetrable past that the passerby can only admire from a vast distance. The firemen were painted in 1957 but, in Murphy's luminous art, they live in a place and time curiously unattached to what the human eye could see in West Tisbury's fire station in that year.

It was Stan Murphy's peculiar genius to create a pictorial world of his own, much as he had once created himself—a modern-day Vermeer of the Vineyard in a nobleman's red hat. A watcher, a dreamer who was also, not coincidentally, a fisherman-farmer-builder-father-friend. An Islander, imbued with the ethos of hard work and fiercely dedicated to keeping some distilled essence of his lovely, magical, mysterious Island alive forever in the plangent tones of blue seas and bright eyes and red hats.

The Plates

Everett Whiting 1950
encaustic on paper
15 ½ X 12
Collection Polly Woollcott Murphy

Farmer and neighbor Everett Whiting is pictured here with his sons, Danny (standing) and Allen (bottom-up in bucket), and with their Border collie, Colin.

Ernest Mayhew 1950

crayon on wood

37 X 29

Collection Chris and Barbara Murphy

Murphy rendered this early drawing of Ernest Mayhew, a local figure whose portrait he would paint in 1958 (p. 35), using Crayola crayons. Due to fading, it was recolored twice, most recently in the fall of 2002.

Chris in Marsh with Black Duck 1955

oil on canvas

35 ½ x 24

Collection Polly Woollcott Murphy

Pictured here at age nine, Chris Murphy, eldest child of Polly and Stan, was born in Baltimore, Maryland, and brought to the Island at the age of two. An avid naturalist and fisherman, he has worked the ponds and shores of Martha's Vineyard all his life. He is married to Barbara Thomas and is the father of Hope and Mary.

Laura and Kitty on the Path to Bannie's 1955
Tri-tec on wood
31 X 22
Collection Polly Woollcott Murphy

The Murphys' two young daughters, who today still live on the Island, contracted Rocky Mountain
spotted fever in 1955. Among the first known victims of the disease in Massachusetts, they nearly died
before a correct diagnosis was made at Massachusetts General Hospital. This painting was begun
while the girls were still in hospital, after it was clear they would survive. Although an artist's notation
on the back of the canvas indicates the medium to have been "oil-casein-wax emulsion," Murphy's
personal record book indicates the medium was Tri-tec, an early polymer acrylic tempera developed by
a Boston artist allergic to oil paint.

Officers of the West Tisbury Fire Department 1957

oil on canvas

40 x 60

Collection Estate of Michael Straight

The officers, from left to right, are: Leonard Athearn, Jack Scannell, Arnold Fischer, Grafton King, and Everett Whiting. It was a volunteer fire department, and Murphy, who wore Badge No. 4, was one of its first members.

Len Athearn with Cows in Stanchions 1958

oil on canvas

22 × 33

Collection Dinah Straight Krosnick

Leonard Athearn, a thirteenth-generation Islander, was a frequent subject of Murphy's paintings.
He is shown here with the dairy cows of Oak Grove Farm, which he ran for many years.
"The farm and its barn were right behind our house," the artist recalled, "and when our children
were little they spent much time there with Leonard."

Biography of Ernest Mayhew 1958

oil on canvas

52 x 40

Collection Polly Woollcott Murphy

Ernest Mayhew was a farmer-fisherman who lived in Chilmark during the first half of the twentieth century. He is remembered locally for his philosophical axiom: "If you can't make a dollar, make fifty cents." Like Roger Allen (p. 45), he knew and used the sign language of the deaf, employed widely in Chilmark, where at one time half the population suffered from hereditary deafness. His barn and house are now part of Chilmark Chocolates, off State Road.

The Murphy Family 1958
oil on panel
46 × 53
Collection Polly Woollcott Murphy

This portrait depicts the Murphy family and pets. David, the youngest child, is on the couch with Polly;
Chris, the eldest, stands behind, while Laura is to the right and Kitty sits in front.
The group is completed by the presence of Mandy, the family's golden retriever, and Max, the cat.

Ike Taylor and Kate 1961
oil on panel
48 X 34
Collection Kate Taylor

Dr. Isaac Taylor was a graduate of Harvard Medical School, dean of the medical school at the University of North Carolina, Chapel Hill, and a fine sailor. His daughter, Kate, who lives on the Island with her family, is a well-known singer-songwriter who also designs jewelry.

Lucy Mitchell 1965
oil on board
29 X 19
Collection Lucy Mitchell

Lucy, who grew up on the Island and frequently posed for Murphy, was eighteen years old at the time of this painting. A well-known artist herself, she lives in West Tisbury with her husband, Rez Williams, also an artist.

Virginia Mazer 1965
oil on board
41 X 31
Collection Mark Mazer

Virginia Mazer was a gifted writer and a close friend of the Murphy family. She and her husband,
Dr. Milton Mazer, moved to West Tisbury with their children, Ruth and Mark, in the early 1960s.
"Virginia loved art and literature and was the easiest model I ever had," Murphy recalled.
"We took a May walk together on the Gay Head beach of Menemsha Pond, where this painting was
conceived. It was down in five days, an abnormally short time for me. It is one of my favorite portraits."

When I was born
you were already long gone.
As a child growing up
you were just the large portrait
always hanging above me.
Its great details,
your strong hands,
your steady gaze,
the weathered shingles,
the large rock as your chair.
Always a part of my life
but never here.
The talks we never had.
Without the portrait
you would simply be
the empty word
Grandfather.

Ned Allen-Posin, grandson

Roger Allen 1966
oil on canvas
46 × 34
Collection Clarissa Allen Posin

A respected contractor and Chilmark selectman, Roger is depicted at the 300-year-old family sheep
farm on South Road. He grew up in Chilmark at a time when everyone used the sign language
of the deaf, which he taught to his daughter and her friends. He is sitting here on the "horse rock," used
by the family women to mount horseback. His daughter, Clarissa, and her family continue to live
on the Allen farm.

Drawing of Sarah Mayhew 1966
pencil on paper
16½ X 13
Private collection

Sarah, daughter of John and Shirley Mayhew of Music Street, grew up in West Tisbury and was
ten years old at the time of this drawing. A photographer currently living in California, she returns to
West Tisbury often and maintains close ties to the Island.

Bill Thomas 1970
pencil on paper
7½ x 5½
Collection Chris and Barbara Murphy

Bill Thomas was born in Oak Bluffs and lived his life there, marrying Mary Reed of New Bedford and raising three children, Anne, Bill, Jr., and Barbara. He worked at the Martha's Vineyard State Forest for many years until his retirement in the early 1970s. An avid golfer, he was a registrar of voters for the town of Oak Bluffs for more than fifty years and active in many community organizations.

Bill Thomas.
Dec. 23, '70
Murphy.

To our dear Barbara · Christmas, 1970.

Norman Benson 1973

oil on door

60 x 40

Collection Leo and Alison Convery

A renowned fisherman on the Island, Captain Benson spent his life on the surrounding waters, usually with his son, Franklin. Together they ran the last fish trap in Buzzard's Bay. This painting shows the captain netting alewife herring in Tisbury Great Pond in the spring of 1973. Benson also wrote a book of stories, *Salt Water in My Veins,* with the assistance of William L. Peltz. He lived to the age of ninety-eight, full of great stories until the end.

Everett Whiting 1977
pencil on paper
18 × 14
Collection The Whiting Family

This drawing shows the process Murphy sometimes used in planning a portrait. The notes clarify certain procedures he followed when he painted, and the drawing can be compared with the finished product in the portrait *The Selectmen of West Tisbury* (p. 55).

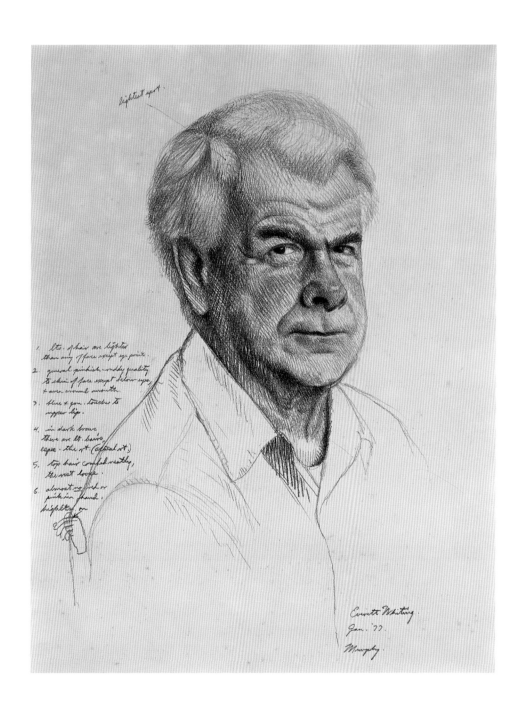

The Selectmen of West Tisbury 1977

oil on door

61 X 41

Collection West Tisbury Town Hall

Allen Look, Everett Whiting, and John Alley are shown on the steps of what was then the West Tisbury Town Hall and is now the police station. Alley, then the junior selectman, served as selectman until 2003. Look and his family lived off Tiah's Cove Road, and Whiting lived at the Whiting farm, where his son Allen (p. 69) now lives.

Claire Duys 1981
oil on canvas
40 X 30
Collection David and Bea Frantz

Claire Duys was born in Switzerland and emigrated to the United States in 1913. Multilingual, she was governess to the children of the Putnam family of New York and Chilmark and first came to the Island with them. Later, she had her own house on Music Street, in West Tisbury. A noted equestrienne and a fine musician, she was first violinist with the Island Symphonetta under Alan Hovey and Hamilton Benz. Mrs. Duys was ninety years old when this picture was painted, and lived to ninety-five.

Hilary and the Oxen 1982
oil on door
36 × 53¾
Collection Chilmark Library

Hilary Blockson, who lives in West Tisbury, bought this pair of retired oxen to teach herself how
to drive a team and to help in her landscape business. The animals, Buck and Shorty, lived out their
natural lives on Brookside Farm, on Middle Road in Chilmark.

Self-Portrait 1984
oil on panel
6 ½ × 5 ¼ inches
Private collection

Tess Bramhall 1984
oil on panel
16 X 12
Collection Tess Bramhall

Tess Bramhall of West Tisbury is a conservationist and a sportswoman who was a member of Murphy's golf foursome for more than twenty years. She is married to the well-known painter Kib Bramhall and for many years was a docent at the Museum of Fine Arts in Boston.

Self-Portrait 1986
oil on canvas
48 x 34
Collection Chris and Barbara Murphy

Mary and Harrison the Crow 1989

oil on door

36 X 24

Collection Mary Murphy Boyd

Mary Murphy Boyd, daughter of Chris and Barbara Murphy, is pictured here with a crow found by her father. Having grown up in Chilmark and attended the Island schools, she graduated Smith College, cum laude, and now teaches in the West Tisbury Elementary School. She has also served as an emergency medical technician on the Island and taken over her father's traditional clambake business. She is married to Jonathan Boyd, a charter fisherman and builder in Chilmark.

Allen Whiting 1990
oil on door
30 X 20
Private collection

Allen Whiting was born on the Island and brought up in West Tisbury on the sheep farm
that has been in his family for generations. An artist, he continues to farm his land, which also
serves as subject and inspiration for his paintings.

Nelson Bryant 1991

oil on canvas, mounted on Masonite

18 ⅛ × 15 ⅝

Private collection

Nelson Bryant came to the Island as a child and lived year-round in West Tisbury. During World War II he was a paratrooper in the 82nd Airborne Division; he was dropped into Normandy on the night before D-Day and wounded in action there. An all-around outdoorsman as well as a writer, he was managing editor of the *Daily Eagle* in Claremont, New Hampshire, before becoming a columnist for the *New York Times*. He continues to live in West Tisbury and to write on outdoor themes for the *Times*.

Jessica Damroth 1991
oil on wood
14 X 12
Collection M. J. Nevin

Jessie Damroth grew up in Chilmark, attended the Menemsha School, and graduated from American University, Phi Beta Kappa, majoring in criminal justice.

JESSICA

Milton Jeffers 1992

oil on wood panel

18 X 14

Collection Estate of M. Anthony Fisher

Milton Jeffers was legendary on Chappaquiddick and in Edgartown as a man who could do anything.
He was an artist, a welder, a fisherman, and a fixer of any and everything. A great storyteller
and a repository of local history, Milton, a member of the Wampanoag tribe, was a friend to all who
appeared on his doorstep.

A Memory of George Cook Trapping Herring 1993

oil on door

16 x 18

Collection Estate of M. Anthony Fisher

A highly respected stone mason and a member of the Wampanoag tribe, George Cook
was also the steward of the herring creek in Aquinnah, where he lived. He is shown here harvesting
the herring at night, a time-honored tradition.

Jim Morgan 1994
oil on canvas
60 X 40
Collection Michael and Carol Van Valkenburgh

Captain Morgan has fished out of Menemsha for years on the dragger *Mary and Verna,* and before
that he worked on other boats, including the Larsens' *Christina* and *Dan.* He is the patriarch
of the Menemsha fishing village and has helped numerous young fishermen. Captain Morgan also
paints nautical scenes and makes weather vanes.

Rez Williams 1994
oil on canvas
32 x 32
Collection Rez Williams

Originally from New York State, Rez Williams has lived in West Tisbury for many years, where
he is an artist and husband to Lucy Mitchell. This painting was inspired by a chance meeting with
Rez at Dysart's, a famous truck stop near Bangor, Maine.

Hershel West and Minnie 1994

oil on canvas

60 x 40

Collection Michael and Carol Van Valkenburgh

A lifelong resident of Chilmark and a colorful denizen of Menemsha, Hershel West fished on his own and often crewed for the Larsens, also of Menemsha. He was involved in the filming of *Jaws* and can be seen in the movie with his elegantly clipped poodle, Minnie, a constant companion.

Chris and Charity 1994
oil on canvas
60 × 44
Private collection

Chris Murphy, the artist's eldest son (pictured as a child, p. 27), appears here with his dog, Charity, on his oyster skiff in Tisbury Great Pond. This portrait is one of three Murphy painted in homage to Chilmark's fishermen during the town's tricentennial year. The related paintings depict fishermen Jim Morgan (p. 79) and Hershel West (p. 83).

Alfred Vanderhoop 1996

oil on canvas

52 × 38

Collection Aquinnah Tribal Council

A Wampanoag tribal elder who often portrayed the mythic giant Moshup in the annual pageant, Alfred Vanderhoop was a fisherman all his life, working the local waters on his boat, the *Redwing,* until his death.

RED WING
AY HEAD MASS

Dan Bryant 1999
oil on canvas
44 × 36
Collection Don and Fan Ogilvie

Danny Bryant of Chilmark is a noted hunter and gatherer also famous for his wit and storytelling ability. He is shown here with his dog, Duchess, on the shores of Black Point Pond, Chilmark.

Bob Flanders 1999
oil on canvas
50 × 39
Private collection

Bob Flanders grew up in Chilmark. A fisherman, carpenter, and carver, among other trades, he remains one of the elders of a large and interesting Island family.

Self-Portrait 2000
oil on canvas
10 x 8
Collection Michael and Carol Van Valkenburgh

Artist's Chronology

Stanley Murphy in his studio, Chilmark, Massachusetts

1922
Born John Stanley Murphy on April 2, the only child of John and Lorraine Murphy, in Saint Paul, Minnesota. Murphy senior sells life insurance, a profession that will take the family to several locations.

1932
Family moves to Buffalo, New York, where young Stan attends Catholic school and serves as a choir boy. He privately repudiates his religion at age twelve.

1934
Family moves to Baltimore, Maryland, where Murphy attends public school and, for his high-school years, the Baltimore Friend's School. It is here that he meets Polly Woollcott, a year his junior. He excels at lacrosse and football and furthers his love of drawing by contributing cartoons, mostly on athletic themes, to the school paper, *The Quaker Quill.*

1940
Murphy wishes to attend art school upon graduation, but his parents object and he begins study at Baltimore Loyola College. He stays only a year, and spends a brief time at the Maryland Institute of Fine and Practical Arts (now Maryland Institute College of Art).

1941
After the attack on Pearl Harbor, Murphy realizes he will have to serve in the military and enrolls at Johns Hopkins University because of the ROTC program there.

1942
Leaves college to enlist in the U. S. Army Infantry. Attends Officer Candidates School and emerges as a second lieutenant.

1945
Marries Polly Woollcott in Little Rock, Arkansas, where he is stationed, and is shipped out for Japan two months later. Although the war ends before he reaches Okinawa, he spends a year there, now as a first lieutenant, as an air courier flying mail to occupied Japan, the Philippines, and other destinations.

1946

Returns to Baltimore, where his first child, Christopher, had been born three months earlier. Polly, knowing of his dream to attend art school, has already enrolled him at the Art Students League in New York, on the recommendation of *Baltimore Sun* cartoonist Edmund Duffy. Attending under the G.I. Bill to study commercial art (a concession to the practical objections of his parents), he moves his young family into veterans' housing: a Quonset hut in Canarsie. He works mostly with lithography and publishes cartoons in *Colliers, Argosy,* and other publications, as well as "spots" (insert drawings) for *The New Yorker,* done for $20 each. He spends time at the Metropolitan Museum of Art and the Frick Collection, however, where he develops a strong attraction to Old Master paintings, especially the works of Rembrandt. He wants to paint, and to leave New York.

1948

Moves to Martha's Vineyard, where Polly had summered with her family in earlier years, and settles in West Tisbury. A second child, Laura, is born

in 1949. To earn a living, Murphy takes a job at Hancock Hardware, where he stocks shelves and makes blueprints. He later takes on part-time work at neighbor Everett Whiting's farm and on construction projects; the couple goes scalloping in the winter and clamming in the summer for additional income. Murphy begins painting in a studio he rents in the top of a barn, training himself in technique by studying from books and traveling to Boston's Museum of Fine Arts to absorb work by Velázquez, Bruegel, van Ruysdael, and others.

1951

Becomes friends with famed painter and Island resident Thomas Hart Benton, whose frequent conversations and encouragement become important to the artist. It is during this period that Murphy travels door-to-door around the Island, offering to create portraits of residents' summer homes. He receives a commission from the prominent stage actress Katharine Cornell. Delighted with the painting (now in the collection of the Dukes County Historical Society), she becomes a patron and introduces his

work to New York philanthropist Adele Levy. Levy later supports the artist for a two-year period, allowing him to devote his time exclusively to painting for a period. Daughter Katharine is born (named after Cornell), and the family moves to Chilmark.

1953

Murphy wishes to apply to an open show at the Metropolitan Museum of Art in New York, but needs backing to take time off for the project. Cornell "pre-buys" a painting from him to enable him to create a work in encaustic, *Dukes County Agricultural Fair;* it becomes one of 400 works chosen from among 6,000 entrants. Son David is born.

1958

Builds a gallery next to his house in Chilmark to display his own work. Enlists Dan Manter to build the first section, for $1,200, and later builds the second section himself. Exhibits of Murphy's work are held annually and, later, biannually in this gallery. Creating landscapes, seascapes, still lifes, portraits, and "fantasy" paintings, he also begins in the early 1960s to paint flower arrangements; their popularity brings income, but he worries they will limit his artistic output. He also creates a series of "Ancestor Portraits," humorous cartoon-painting self-portraits in various historical settings and garb, portraying himself as a cardinal, a caveman, a Japanese warrior, and an Irish monk, among others.

Throughout his many years in the community, he serves as an inaugural volunteer member of the West Tisbury Fire Department, on the school committee and other town boards in Chilmark, and as a board member and two-term co-chair of the Martha's Vineyard Historical Society.

1968

The Murphy family moves back to neighboring West Tisbury. Murphy continues to engage passionately in duck hunting, lobstering, and shellfishing. Plays both the guitar and piano and furthers his love of opera, classical music, and jazz.

1971

Receives commission to paint four canvas murals that are installed on the wall of the Katharine Cornell Theatre, above the Vineyard Haven Town Hall. The paintings depict Island themes: the whaling era, a Menemsha fishing village, a beach scene, and the native Wampanoag tale of the giant Moshup and the Gay Head Cliffs, said to be imprinted with a hundred million years of history.

1978

After years spent amassing a fine collection of duck decoys, publishes book *Decoys of Martha's Vineyard* (1978, David R. Godine), still the definitive work on this subject.

In the 1970s, Murphy abandons painting portraits on commission and opts in his later years to paint only subjects he wishes to portray.

2002

Murphy is awarded the Ruth J. Bogan Memorial Fund's 2001 Creative Living Award by the Committee for the Permanent Endowment Fund of Martha's Vineyard.

Retrospective exhibition *Fifty Years of Island Portraits* held in August in honor of the artist's eightieth year. The exhibition brings together works in portraiture from across his career, and Murphy attends the opening, putting in his first appearance at an exhibition of his work in fifty years. He begins the planning for a book that documents the work in the exhibition.

2003

Dies on July 23. Memorial service in his honor held in August.